TRANSFORMING YOUR LIFE

Michael Hurley

Transforming Your Life

A PARTICIPANT'S HANDBOOK

the columba press

First published in 1998 by
the columba press
55a Spruce Avenue, Stillorgan Industrial Park
Blackrock, Co Dublin

Cover by Bill Bolger
Origination by The Columba Press
Printed in Ireland by Colour Books Ltd, Dublin

This booklet is for the use of participants in the *Come and See* course
which is outlined in
Transforming Your Parish by Michael Hurley

ISBN 1 85607 227 4

Contents

Introduction

Bill is from Donegal. He has worked all his life in a high profile job in the public sector. Four years ago he took early retirement because he wanted time to play golf. Today he smiles wryly as he recounts why golf now has a very secondary place in his life. Together with his wife, Patricia, he leads a small faith-sharing group which is based in their home. He seeks every opportunity to place his gifts at the service of the local community. He never believed that retirement could be so exciting.

Josephine is a young mother who would be the first to admit that in the past she had been very shy. Some time ago I heard her speak at a Sunday Mass with great clarity and enthusiasm about her meetings with children ranging in age from nine to thirteen. She explained how these children had learned to pray spontaneously and had become so much more confident and happy.

Jenny is 21 years of age. Six years ago she began sharing her faith with other young people of her own age. She formed a youth faith group, who have continued to meet together every two weeks up to the present time. They enjoy being with one another. They laugh a lot. The primary reason they meet is to reflect and share on where they see God in their lives. They pray for one another when there are personal difficulties. A few years ago this group was trained to run retreats and make presentations to young people through mime, drama, song and personal story. Today Jenny is a catechist and teaches religion in a secondary school.

It all began for Bill, Josephine and Jenny when they attended the course, *Come and See*, as you are about to do. They
are three of hundreds who found that it was the beginning
of something new for them. I will let three others state
what it meant for them:

> 'I recommended so many people to do the course. It
> was a beginning for me. It opened up the whole
> thing about God and faith. I made so many real
> friends' (Dymphna).

> 'It was an opportunity I had been waiting for. It was
> a great preparation for Easter. It gave me a great
> sense of peace. I was able to step out of the hassle of
> life and find a hope and meaning in knowing that
> God was with me and that he loved me. I received so
> much. I then wanted to give something back so I be-
> came a group leader the next time around' (Derek).

> 'It was like God woke up in my life. Something came
> alive. God became real for me as a friend. I still think
> I don't have a very good faith, but now I stop to give
> thanks to God' (Bernadette).

David Barrett in the *World Christian Encyclopaedia* claims
that 'The world is more religious than ever; almost every
kind of religion has come back as a decisive factor in
human life.' We can see the truth of this by a visit to any religious bookshop, with its vast array of tapes, videos,
books and magazines. There is a new interest in Eastern re-
ligions. There is the rapid growth of new religious move-
ments. There is also the explosion in non-Christian litera-
ture promising meaning and fulfilment. There is the
human potential movement, claiming that we can heal
ourselves, and that we carry within us the destiny of our
own lives without any reference to a personal God. Where
the church is not making available the richness of its life, it
runs the risk of being left on the sidelines. People will not
look to it to meet their needs for belonging, meaning and

healing. Sadly, we can already see so much evidence of this happening.

The value of *Come and See* is precisely that it looks at fundamental aspects of our Catholic faith. The first meeting looks at the world in which we live. We are at a time of great change, and this calls for a new faith response from us. We are to be pioneers, who need to learn again an ability to speak about our faith amid the questions raised by those we meet. The second meeting takes up the theme of evangelisation, of sharing one's faith, which has been central to the teaching of Pope John Paul II. The third helps us to do this as we relate to people in our homes, neighbourhoods and places of work. The next looks at the richness of our baptism and leads to a personal conviction about the love of Jesus Christ for each one as a child of the Father. The final meeting treats of the support that is needed to live a Christian life with enthusiasm and joy.

A Vision for Your Life

Come and See will seek to communicate God's vision for your life. It sees faith as a gift from God, which has been nurtured and shaped though your relationships and the events of your life. You will be invited to take a responsibility for this gift. You will be prompted to make a new decision for Christ. In reality, this is accepting your baptism as an adult. Very likely baptism was something that 'happened' to you as a child. Now you can make it your own. You really *are* a child of God. You are part of his people, giving and receiving help within his church. Jesus offers you new life. You too receive 'power when the Holy Spirit comes upon you' (Acts 1:8). Faith is intended to make a difference in your life, a gift that is given to enrich you as a person. Equally it is to impact the world around you through the example of your life and through your words. 'Then you will be my witnesses' (Acts 1:8).

We are not doing too well today as a church in witnessing, in what Pope John Paul II calls exercising our 'supreme duty' (*RM* 3). Fr Alvin Illig, director of the Paulist National Evangelisation Association in the USA, estimates that less than 2% of a typical Catholic congregation have an evangelising attitude. In other words, 98% relate to the church as to a spiritual filling station, where they can commune in a private way with God. Faith, then, is a pious activity. It is a seeking of personal peace in the saying of prayers. At its extreme, this can be the constant quest for new 'religious' experiences, or reliance on the great comforter to escape the pain of living, while not addressing issues. We end up with 'over-eating' and 'over-weight' Catholics, whose continuing demand is for new experiences, extra Masses, more novenas and possibly private revelations. Sharing faith is not a top priority. We stay in the safety of a 'private' faith and lament that so many of our children and even adults do not relate to the church. The course encourages us to be people of faith who seek to live that faith with enthusiasm. Faith originally meant being in God, being filled with God. He still wants to speak to the people of today. His way of doing it is through those who are in touch with him and who know his influence in their lives.

What you can expect

A lot of preparation will have gone into this *Come and See*. Those organising it will be delighted to see you attend. Nothing is as bad as to set something up and then no one to arrive. They will want you to benefit from it and to enjoy it. So do express your appreciation for their efforts. Make up your mind to enter into it and to enjoy it.

You will join in singing a hymn or two if you know them. You will not be expected to say anything publicly unless you wish to do so. A scripture passage will be read. There follows a time of silence. Then anyone who wishes to make a comment may do so. Usually three or four mention something that drew their attention in the passage read.

The small group can appear somewhat intimidating for some. It is important to realise that this is not the time nor place to share great personal details. The purpose of the small group is to offer a time of reflection on the talk you have heard and to insure that each person can take most from it. Two or three questions based on the talk are set for discussion. Each person is then encouraged to make personal responses to the questions asked. You will not be expected to say anything more than you consider 'safe' in this setting. In fact you may wish to say very little. It is impressed on the guide within the group to listen with reverence to each person as they speak and to welcome each opinion. They are not present as experts but as fellow pilgrims (most likely fellow parishioners) with you.

The value of these small groups is that you learn from

the insights of one another. It will show you the great vari-
ety of ways of seeing the same question. It also has the
value of giving you the opportunity of speaking about
faith. At the end of each course, people often draw attention to the importance of the group. They become more at
home with speaking about faith. They form a close bond
with the others present. They appreciate the other view-
points shared which cause them to think differently. It
often surprises them to hear someone they already know
speak about the importance of God or prayer in his/her
life. It encourages them when they hear of the faith and the
struggle of another.

People usually experience apprehension when they are
undertaking something new or are entering a new situation. This will probably be true for some who gather for
the course. It evaporates very quickly as people are wel-
comed and begin to get to know each other.

What you may experience:
In the creed we declare that we believe in 'the Holy Spirit,
the Lord, the giver of life'. He gives life. Our hope and
prayer is that you become more aware of the mystery that
God is in your life and that you will know the mysterious
power and influence of his Spirit and be surprised. You
can expect a deepening of faith. You will be encouraged to
take on a greater responsibility for this great gift. This will
be your likely response to the song, prayer, scripture and
teaching that will be part of each night. A lot of preparation has been put into this course to ensure that it will be a
happy and fruitful event for you. There has been much
prayer, a number of meetings, a lot of thought and plan-
ning. You should experience a friendly atmosphere. There
will grow a sense of belonging to one another and to the
parish as you will be with people who are searching together for meaning and for truth. You will make a number
of good friends.

You will learn to speak to God in a more personal way. You will be encouraged to take time each day to pray. These will be the moments when you commune alone with God. Here you will find a deepening of a sense of his love for you and of his plan for you life. This is seen as an important part of the course. It will be important to decide on a time and to find a reasonably comfortable place where you know you will not be disturbed. What happens on Sunday, and at the course, will simply be words unless you relate with him in the silence and complexities of your life. Jesus said very little about prayer, except to encourage his followers to pray. One learns to pray by doing it. You will be with people who wish to take God more seriously. This will be a great inspiration to you. On occasion one of the leaders or a guide will say a prayer. You will also find this most helpful as it will indicate how another prays. Remember there is no one way to pray. You will find your way.

The scriptures will open up to you as the Word of God. Many have found the section 'Living Words' helpful as a basis for prayer. In your quiet time, ask God to speak to you through the passage assigned for the particular day. It is his word. Then read it. After some silence, read it again. Allow yourself to be drawn to a phrase or thought in it. At times it happens that you may think it has said very little, yet later during the day it comes to mind as being especially relevant to a particular situation or event. This is the word of God for you. You can expect that most of the passages will speak very directly and clearly to you. It is intended that at the end of the course you will have a conviction about the scriptures and a facility in opening the Bible and using it in prayer.

The gift of faith will become more than ever good news for you. You will see a richer meaning in many of the prayers and values that were important to you. Thus you will be more confident in engaging in dialogue with others who may have very different perspectives. Comfortable in your own identity, you will no longer see the need to win arguments, but will relate to all on the basis of respect. You will find that the most obvious difference it will make will be within your own home. You will be alert to opportunities in passing on faith. You will see each as a child of God. You may have a greater confidence in working through the school religious programme with your children and in encouraging a family time of reflection. I know of one parent whose children, all young adults, no longer attend Mass. She now admits that she relates to them no longer on the basis that they should attend, but rather at the level of the values that are important to them. This, she claims, has been the value of the course for her. It has enabled her to speak with them about values and to offer her own story of the influence of God in her life. You may experience the challenge of how your faith can best make a difference as you relate to others and to the world around you.

You will learn of the influence of the Holy Spirit. The Holy Spirit was experienced as gift in the early church and throughout the history of our people. Their only explanation was that this was God's unearned and unmerited goodness to them. They witnessed its effects. 'The Spirit makes us cry out, "Abba, Father". The Spirit himself and our spirit bear united witness that we are children of God' (Rom 8:15-16). The Spirit brought them into a living relationship with God, and inspired spontaneous worship and praise.

Throughout the New Testament there are a number of lists of gifts, not intended to be exhaustive, of the Holy Spirit. They are called manifestations and demonstrations of the Spirit. We find them in 1 Corinthians 12:7-11, 28-30; Ephesians 4; Romans 12:7; and 1 Peter 4. The gifts given by the Spirit included the message of faith and of knowledge, healing, miraculous powers, prophecy, tongues, leadership, hospitality, evangelism, pastoring, administration, and teaching. The community was given life through the Spirit. It made it distinctive from every other grouping. It was not a democracy. Rather the Spirit inspired gifts in each person. Each then served the others and heralded the good news according to God's grace at work in their lives. The community was mystical, comprising those who had experienced the Spirit of the Risen Lord, who were inspired by his gifts, and were offering them in service.

This being gifted was seen as having three purposes for the early church:

a) to lead to a deeper faith in God.
b) to build community, to build up the Body of Christ.
c) to awaken a disinterested world.

The world is already tired of words. It needs the demonstration that Christianity works. It looks for signs of God's presence in lives converted by him, as seen in the way believers love one another and in their care and love for the poor. It is the Spirit who gives words to those who seek to declare for him before others. It is he who prompts coincidences, signs, and awakenings in the hearts of those who hear. It was such in the early church. It is to be the norm too for today.

Conclusion

I am delighted that you have decided to undertake *Come and See*. May it be the beginning of an exciting journey for you. After this series of meetings, you may wish to make some new decisions. They will come solely as yours, whatever they may be. It will not even be necessary to declare what they are. They may be about working at some primary relationship in your life, without any further involvement in groups or within the parish. Alternatively, you may wish to undertake some parish service in response to a need you observe. The leaders will help you should that be your decision. Some may wish to continue with some form of supportive network. Again the leaders will help in making this a reality for you.

After completing the course, you may like to read the final chapter of this booklet where I give some details of the workings of the cell groups. They may offer some pointers as to what may be possible in your own situation.

One thing is certain. God is nearer to us than we realise. Our ancestors knew this: '*Is giorra cabhair Dé ná an doras*' (God's help is closer than the door). He now has more in store for you than you may expect. A traditional prayer expresses well what our expectation can be:

Come, Holy Spirit, fill the hearts of your faithful
and enkindle in them the fire of your love.
Send forth your Spirit and they shall be recreated
and thou shall renew the face of the earth.

Living Words

Personal Prayer during the course

Introduction

Prayer is creating an atmosphere where life is simplified. In prayer, we bring to God, who is love, all the joys and hardships which crowd in upon us. Prayer has many moods: some times we are presenting our struggles, some times we are expressing our gratitude for God's goodness. But always prayer is a conversation in which we take on a trusting, childlike attitude before God in the certainty of his love and providence.

Living Words offer a scripture passage and a brief reflection for each day of *Come and See*. Week 1, Day 1 is for the day after you have begun the course. The thoughts for each week are linked to the themes of your meetings.

Decide on a precise time for your daily prayer and select a comfortable place where you are unlikely to be disturbed. You may like to start with a few moments simply to become quiet. Then make a short prayer that the Spirit of God will guide you during your time with him. Read the scripture passage through and then, after a period of silence, read it a second time, allowing it to become for you a living word. The reflection is simply an aid to this prayer. You may then like to conclude with a prayer of thanksgiving for what you have heard, and to invite God to help you in living out his word during the rest of the day.

WEEK 1

Day 1:
Unbind him, let him go free (Jn 11:44).
Listen today to the voice and the mind of Christ as he speaks to you in your particular situation.

Day 2:
There was no water for the people to drink. So they grumbled against Moses (Ex 17:1). Yahweh said to Moses: 'You yourselves have seen what I did with the Egyptians, how I carried you on eagle's wings and brought you to myself. From this you know that now, if you obey my voice and hold fast to my covenant, you of all the nations shall be my very own for all the earth is mine. I will count you a kingdom of priests, a consecrated nation.' Then Moses informed all the elders of the people and all the people answered as one. 'All that Yahweh has said, we will do' (Ex 19:4-8).
It was a time of constant change for the people of Israel as they continued their journey out of slavery towards the promised land. They forgot about God's guidance of, and of his faithfulness to, them. They forgot how much he was on their side. Instead they grumbled and complained. They blamed Moses. Amid the complaints, the accusations and the uncertainties of today, you too can rely on God's faithfulness. He remains faithful to you. He is calling you to himself. Let his word for you this day speak to your heart.

Day 3:
The master praised the dishonest steward for his astuteness. For the children of this world are more astute in dealing with their own kind than are the children of light (Lk 16:8).
People put so much time, effort and talent into personal

promotion and advancement and into the attainment of material goals. How much more should we place our giftedness and energy at the service of God for the building of his kingdom?

Day 4:

It is God, for his own loving purpose, who puts both the will and the action into you. Do all that has to be done without complaining or arguing and then you will be innocent and genuine, perfect children of God among a deceitful and underhand brood, and you will shine in the world like bright stars, because you are offering it the word of life (Phil 2:13-16).

God is at work in your life. He is inspiring in you a prayer, a generosity, and a wish to serve him. As you seek to serve him faithfully, he has promised that you will be a light for him in the world and you will be offering others the opportunity to find new life in him. Give thanks to God who is near. Thank him for who you are at this time in your life.

Day 5:

You must keep to what you have taught and know to be true: remember who your teachers were and how, ever since you were a child, you have known the holy scriptures – from these you can learn the wisdom that leads to salvation through faith in Christ Jesus. All scripture is inspired by God and can profitably be used for teaching, for refuting error, for guiding people's lives and teaching them to be holy. This is how the one who is dedicated to God becomes fully equipped and ready for any good work (2 Tim 3:14-17).

'Ignorance of scripture is ignorance of Christ' (St Jerome). The scriptures are God's word for your life. They are God's gift to you so that you can come to know him and also to be equipped to work effectively with him. So let his words seep into the deepest parts of your life.

Today thank God for your 'teachers'. Recall, with gratitude, those who have influenced you, those who have
been your role models through the example of their lives,
through their words, and above all through the love you
knew they had for you.

Day 6:

Make your home in me, as I make mine in you. As a
branch cannot bear fruit by itself, but must remain
part of the vine, neither can you unless you remain
in me. I am the vine, you are the branches. Whoever
remains in me, with me in him, bears fruit in plenty;
for cut off from me you can do nothing. I commis-
sioned you to go out and to bear fruit that will last
(Jn 15:4-5, 16).

Jesus calls us to make a difference and to bear fruit. He invites us to remain close to him and to a deeper trust in him.
Then we are to let our faith impact the culture and the relationships within which we operate. Our faith is not to be
dormant and passive.

Day 7:

For the mountains may depart, the hills be shaken,
but my love for you will never leave you and my
covenant of peace with you will never be shaken,
says Yahweh who takes pity on you (Is 54:10).

Oh, come to the water all you who are thirsty;
though you have no money, come!
Buy corn without money, and eat,
and, at no cost, wine and milk (Is 55:1).

You may think that your resources are little – that you
have little to give. You may think that you have few answers for the issues and difficulties of life. You may think
that you are helpless in the face of much that happens
around you and to you. You may even feel empty and dry,
with little zest for life. Well, listen again to God's word for
you. He is making promises to you.

WEEK 2

Day 1:

Philip said to Nathaniel: 'We have found the one Moses wrote about in the Law, the one about whom the prophets wrote: he is Jesus, son of Joseph, from Nazareth'. 'From Nazareth?' said Nathaniel, 'Can anything good come from that place?' 'Come and see,' replied Philip (Jn 1:45-46).

One friend invites another. The discovery of good news is followed by inviting family and friends to share in it. When you wish to pass on faith to others, what are you inviting them to come and see? To come and see the relationship of friendship that Jesus desires to have with them? To come and see where Christianity is lived and where people find support to live with deep faith? In your prayer today ask for the grace that you can take the place of Philip as you relate to your family and friends. Listen to the promptings of Christ in your life and hear his vision for your life.

Day 2:

All authority in heaven and on earth has been given to me. Go, therefore, make disciples of all the nations; baptise them in the name of the Father and of the Son and of the Holy Spirit, and teach them to observe all the commands I gave you. And know that I am with you always; yes, to the end of time (Mt 28:18-20).

Jesus is commanding his disciples to look outwards. He is sending them with his authority to be active and to make disciples. To whom are you being sent with the authority of Christ? Who are in your world? You are meeting them each day as you go about your daily work. You evangelise as you go; you don't need to go to evangelise. In your prayer today bring before the Lord those whom you meet

each day, pray for the gift of love for each of them and for
the gift of courage to be able to sensitively speak words of
faith at opportune times.

Day 3:

You will receive power when the Holy Spirit comes
on you, and then you will be my witnesses not only
in Jerusalem but throughout Judaea and Samaria,
and indeed to the ends of the earth (Acts 1:8).

'There can be no evangelisation without the co-oper-
ation of the Holy Spirit ... He suggests to every
preacher of the gospel the right words which he
alone could provide and at the same time predisposes
the minds of the hearers to a full acceptance of the
gospel ... we urge all the heralds of the gospel, whatever be their order or rank, to pray unceasingly to
the divine Spirit with faith and ardour and to submit
themselves prudently to his guidance as the principal author of their plans, of their initiatives and their
work in the field of evangelisation' (*EN* 75).

The Lord wishes to empower you with a new gift of the
Holy Spirit to reach others in his name.

Day 4

The rulers, elders and scribes called them in and gave
them a warning on no account to make statements or to
teach in the name of Jesus. But Peter and John retorted,
'You must judge whether in God's eyes it is right to listen
to you and not to God. We cannot promise to stop pro-
claiming what we have seen and heard' (Acts 4:18-20).

The present world may not seem to want to give a place to
the message of Christ. Can you dare to ask God for the
conviction, confidence and courage that you see in Peter
and John?

Day 5:

Not that I boast of preaching the gospel, since it is a duty which has been laid on me: I should be punished if I did not preach it! (1 Cor 9:16)

Baptism and confirmation make us part of God's people and empower us to be witnesses. It is a privilege to be an evangelist. It is to be graced and gifted by God for mission. Paul seeks every opportunity to announce the good news of Jesus Christ. He gives thanks to God by living out the privilege that was his as evangelist and witness. Otherwise God's grace lies dormant.

Day 6:

They will not ask the Lord's help unless they believe in him, and they will not believe in him unless they have heard of him, and they will not hear of him unless they get a preacher, and they will never have a preacher unless one is sent (Rom 10:14-15).

The only gospel that some people will read or see may be what they observe in the example of your life and hear from the words of your lips. Your witness will encourage others to call upon the name of the Lord.

Day 7:

Paul and Barnabas stayed on for some time, preaching fearlessly for the Lord: and the Lord supported all they said about his gift of grace, allowing signs and wonders to be performed by them (Acts 14:3).

It is always a risk to share your faith. It may (and you may) not be understood. You may feel that you know very little and may be 'found out', if the other responds and asks for a deeper understanding of faith. But your confidence is not in what *you* know but in God. He promises that when you take risks for him, you will be supported. You will be given his wisdom in difficult situations: 'I myself shall give you an eloquence and a wisdom that none of your opponents will be able to resist or contradict' (Lk 21:15).

WEEK 3

This week you will write your Good News story. Decide now on a time.

Day 1:

We have seen the Lord (Jn 20:25).

In the scriptures there are many examples of the Lord meeting people in a personal way that takes account of their personal histories – to the disciples, who were filled with fear, he offered peace: 'Peace be with you'; to Thomas, who needed physical touch and proof, he showed his hands and his side; to the two disciples, who knew the Old Testament, he explained the prophecies in the scriptures about Jesus; to Mary, who was alone and lonely, he called by name; to Paul, a strong and independent personality, he stopped him in his tracks on the road so that he then had to be taken by the hand by his companions. Invite God's Spirit to guide you in a review of your life to see his personal love and guidance for you. Thank him for the times you can say: 'I have seen the Lord.'

Day 2:

From Paul, apostle of Christ Jesus to Timothy, true child of mine in the faith; wishing you grace, mercy and peace from God the Father and from Christ Jesus our Lord (1 Tim 1:1-2).

Paul had great affection for Timothy. God sends people into our lives. Thank God for the significant people in your life, who have influenced you to be a person of faith. In them you can see God's goodness to you. They, too, are very likely central in your faith story.

Day 3:

Many Samaritans of that town had believed in him on the strength of the woman's testimony when she said, 'He told me all I have ever done', so, when the Samaritans came up to him, they begged him to stay with them (Jn 4:39-40).

The influence of one's testimony is evident. Once the Samaritan woman had experienced living water in the life of Jesus, and knew of his acceptance and love for her, the people of the town heard her story of conviction and truth. They now knew that they, too, could come to Jesus and 'beg' him to stay with them and to give them living waters. The woman's story stirred up a curiosity in others to seek and to find Jesus.

Day 4:

And their eyes were opened and they recognised him; but he had vanished from their sight. Then they said to each other, 'Did not our hearts burn within us as he talked to us on the road and explained the scriptures to us?' They set out that instant and returned to Jerusalem. There they found the eleven assembled together with their companions, who said to them, 'Yes, it is true. The Lord has risen and has appeared to Simon.' Then they told their story of what had happened on the road and how they had recognised him at the breaking of bread (Lk 24:31-35).

'They set out that instant.' One can almost pick up their enthusiasm and excitement. They wanted to tell their story. Who may you tell your story to today? How may your story be a help to another to live life with greater trust and love of the Lord? In your time of prayer, bring these questions to him. Pray daily for an opportunity to share your story for his glory.

Day 5:

Blessed be the God and Father of our Lord Jesus Christ, a gentle Father and the God of all consolation, who comforts us in all our sorrows, so that we can offer others in their sorrows the consolation that we have received from God ourselves (2 Cor 1:3-4).

There are many elements in one's good news story. One of

them is knowing the comforting love and providence of
God during a time of trial. Let your prayer rise in praise
and gratitude to God for his faithfulness even when you
have been unfaithful to him; for his mercy when you have
wandered from him, and for his comfort and healing at
times of great trauma. Ask the Lord to gently lead you to
specific reasons for praise and gratitude.

Day 6:

We all fell to the ground, and I heard a voice saying
to me, 'Saul, Saul, why are you persecuting me?'
(Acts 26:14).

Paul declared in explanation of his conversion event:
'After that, King Agrippa, I could not disobey the
heavenly vision' (Acts 26:19).

The desire to share one's testimony is a gift. It is like an influence from within, seeking opportunities to make the
good news available to others. It is not a burden, even
when it means risks, misunderstandings, and difficulties.
It is part of who one is; an attitude towards others that
they may experience the love of God and the support of
his people.

Day 7:

I am reminding you now to fan into a flame the gift
that God gave you when I laid my hands on you.
God's gift was not a spirit of timidity, but the Spirit
of power, and love, and self-control. So you are never
to be ashamed of witnessing to the Lord (2 Tim).

In your time of quiet prayer, allow the Lord to fan into a
flame the influence of his Spirit that is within you. Then
you will have greater confidence and power in witnessing
and in living a Christian life.

WEEK 4

Day 1:

As Jesus went along, he saw a man who had been
blind from birth (Jn 9:1).

Thank God for who you are. You are a child of God. He
knows you deeply and accepts you as you are, with all
your imperfections and failings. Thank him for the gift of
his Son, Jesus, who heals you of the wounds and sinful-
ness that are part of you life. Thank him for the gift of his
Spirit, who makes all things new, and is offering you new
beginnings. Expect God to inspire gratitude and praise in
your prayer today.

Day 2:

I have come so that you may have life and have it to
the full (Jn 10:10).

Be present to God as you are. Let God be present to you
face to face. Accept his healing and forgiving love upon
your life or upon a particular area that is surfacing as worry-
ing for you at this time. Hear him call you forth to a full-
ness of life.

Day 3:

God raised this man Jesus to life, and all of us are witnesses to that. Now raised to the heights by God's
right hand, he has received from the Father the Holy
Spirit who was promised, and what you see and
hear is the outpouring of that Spirit (Acts 2:33-34).

As part of your prayer time today say slowly the following
prayer, continuing to seek God's control in your life:

Lord Jesus Christ, I thank you for all you have done
for me. I thank you for suffering death from the
depth of your love for me. I rejoice that you are
raised up in glory at the right hand of the Father.

I thank you for the gift of your Spirit. Your Spirit was

not a gift for the early church alone, but is for me now as I open my hands and my heart to you in prayer. Send forth your Spirit upon me. Let me experience the outpouring of your Spirit that I may know a conversion of my heart, a forgiveness of my sin, a desire to give my life to you and a confidence in knowing you as Lord of my life. Let there be a new Pentecost now in my life.

I know you always want me to expect great things from you and to bear fruit for your glory. Let all I say and do be ever directed by your promptings. Lead me to rediscover my roots in you and among your people, the church

Into your hands I commend my spirit for I trust in your love and providence for me. I bless and thank you for hearing my prayer, which I have made in Christ the Lord. Amen.'

Day 4:

For the Lord Yahweh says this: I am going to look after my flock myself and keep all of it in view ... I will feed them in good pasturage ... I myself will pasture my sheep. I myself will show them where to rest. I shall look for the lost one, bring back the stray, bandage the wounded and make the weak strong. I shall watch over the fat and healthy. I shall be a true shepherd to them (Ezek 34:11,14,15-16).

What extraordinary promises! Be present today to the Lord who speaks these promises to you as he seeks to gather a people who will know his care and love for them. Listen to his call to place your total trust in him. Hear him teach you about what it means to shepherd those whom you meet.

Day 5:

As for human approval, this means nothing to me ...

How can you believe, since you look to one another
for approval and are not concerned with the approval that comes from the one God? (Jn 5:41,44).

Jesus was single-minded. His life's purpose was to discern
the Father's initiatives and to be prepared to pay the price
of co-operating with the Father to establish the reign of
God.

Appearances, what others may think of us and say
about us, and what may bring us benefit in the sight of
others, greatly influence what we say and do. What are the
influences and 'gods' that guide your life? Be specific in
seeking the help and grace you need to live like Jesus, who
always sought the approval that comes from God.

Day 6:

It is by grace that you have been saved, through
faith; not by anything of your own, but by a gift from
God; not by anything that you have done, so that nobody can claim the credit. We are God's work of art,
created in Christ Jesus to live the good life as from
the beginning he had meant us to live it (Eph 2:8-10).

God's grace is ever new. This is a privileged moment of his
grace for you. It is all God's work. You cannot claim the
credit for he has opened your eyes to the mystery of his
greatness and he calls you to make him known in the mar-
ket place. Let a prayer of gratitude and praise surface in
your life.

Day 7:

I tell you, there is rejoicing among the angels of God
over one repentant sinner (Lk 15:10).

It is easier to think of your own efforts than to think of
God's delight and joy in you as you make, with his grace,
the smallest gesture towards him. Did you ever think that
he took great delight in you as he saw you coming today?
You may experience joy when you know his delight in

you. Joy is a fruit of the Spirit. It is the natural condition of those who know that God's love enfolds them and that he takes delight in them.

> The greatest honour we can give to Almighty God is to live gladly because of the knowledge of his love ... We are his bliss, because he endlessly delights in us; and so with his grace shall we delight in him. (Julian of Norwich: *Revelations of Divine Love*)

WEEK 5

Day 1:

They remained faithful to the teaching of the apostles, to the fellowship, to the breaking of bread and to the prayers. They went as a body to the Temple every day but met in their houses for the breaking of bread. Day by day the Lord added to their community (Acts 2:42, 46, 47).

Here we have some of the central elements of the life of the early church – faithful to, and learning from, the teaching of the apostles; a focus on the formation of community, caring for those in need; coming together for worship and for Eucharist. All this was based on the temple, and equally on the home as 'a domestic church'. Growth was part of its life. This, too, is a 'check list' for you as you come before the Lord. Thank him for the ways you live those elements and ask his discernment and grace to help you with those you tend to overlook or to which you do not give sufficient attention.

Day 2:

Where two or three meet in my name, I am there with them (Mt 18:20).

There is a real presence of Christ when you meet with people in his name, whether it be with your family, friends or in a prayer gathering with acquaintances. Bring before the Lord today your prayer for a deeper Christian fellowship, where he will be recognised and where you will receive support in your journey with him.

Day 3:

But you are a chosen race, a royal priesthood, a consecrated nation, a people set apart to sing the praises of God who called you out of darkness into his wonderful light. Once you were not a people at all and

now you are the People of God; once you were out-
side the mercy and now you have been given mercy
(1 Pet 2:9-10).

You have a song to sing; you have praises to express. God
calls you to sing his praises from among the people he is
forming and calling together. God is calling you to people-
hood, to be part of, and to be involved with, his people.
God calls people as individuals to the experience of community with others. Put your roots down amid the new
thing God is doing; amid the people God is calling to a living faith. Lift up your heart and voice in praise of God.

Day 4:

Let the message of Christ, in all its richness, find a
home with you. Teach each other, and advise each
other, in all wisdom. With gratitude in your heart
sing psalms and hymns and inspired songs to God;
and never say or do anything except in the name of
the Lord Jesus, giving thanks to God the Father
through him (Col 3:16-17).

A saint is sometimes described as one whose inner convic-
tions conforms to what is expressed in word and action. It
is to let the message of Christ find a home in you and then
seek to live accordingly. Why should you meet to share
faith with others and what will you do when you meet? In
this passage you find clear guidelines: taking time to let
the message of Christ sink in; sharing wisdom with one
another; expressing gratitude; giving thanks; being led by
the Lord.

Allow the Lord to dream in your thoughts today as you
pray.

Day 5:

'It is not right,' the father-in-law of Moses said to
him, 'to take this on yourself. You will tire yourself
out, you and the people with you. The work is too

heavy for you. You cannot do it alone. Take my advice and God will be with you. You ought to represent the people before God and bring their disputes to him. Teach them the statutes and the decisions; show them the way they must follow and what their course must be. But choose from the people at large some capable and God-fearing ones, trustworthy and incorruptible, and appoint them as leaders of the people: leaders of thousands, hundreds, fifties, tens. Let these be at the service of the people to administer justice at all times. They can refer all difficult questions to you, but all smaller questions they will decide for themselves, so making things easier for you and sharing the burden with you. If you do this – and may God so command you – you will be able to stand the strain, and all these people will go home satisfied' (Ex 18:16-23).

The experience of many people in ministry is that of Moses. In extreme cases it is called 'burnout', due to excessive demands and expectations. Also many people feel that the church does not care for them. It remains too distant for them as they feel they belong to a great anonymous crowd, rather than to a community. In this scripture a clear role for spiritual leaders is outlined. They are to come before God for their people. They are to be their teachers towards wisdom. They are to select and train many leaders to be guides and to care for others. Their strategy then is to place all the people into small groups, with a trained leader. Instead of displacing the person with responsibility, the decisions and matters of consequence will be referred back to him/her. There will be less burdens, with more time for coming before the Lord in intercession for others. All the while people are being provided for, with many taking on some responsibility. What may the Lord be saying to you about all this as a strategy of renewal?

Day 6:

Now you together are Christ's body; but each of you is a different part of it. In the church, God has given the first place to apostles, the second to prophets, the third to teachers; after them, miracles, and after them the gift of healing, helpers, good leaders, those with many languages. Are all of them apostles, or all of them prophets, or all of them teachers? Do they all have the gift of miracles, or all have the gift of healing? Do all speak strange languages, and all interpret them? (1 Cor 12:27-30).

It may also be helpful to read verses 4 to 13.

The witness of any community is much greater than the individual witness of all its members. The body of Christ and each community is called together by God. The Spirit of God inspires a multiplicity of gifts for the community's organisation but especially that it may impact the prevailing culture through miracles, inspired teaching, interpreting the events and trends of the day (prophecy), words of faith, healing, etc. A community is effective when each person offers their own giftedness, whatever that is, as inspired by the Spirit. There is no room for jealousy, only listening to the Spirit of God and encouragement of one another. Entrust your life to the Spirit of God, and seek his guidance in the areas where you are looking for answers.

Day 7:

After this the Lord appointed seventy-two others and sent them out ahead of him, in pairs, to all the towns and places he himself was to visit. He said to them, 'The harvest is rich but the labourers are few, so ask the Lord of the harvest to send labourers to his harvest. Start off now' (Lk 10:1-3).

Do you know that you are being sent from a community to prepare the ground, to break a furrow, so that the Lord can come and reveal his presence? To whom are you being sent? From what community and base are you being sent? With whom will you go?

In your time of prayer today, dream the Lord's dream for you and be attentive to the promptings of his Spirit for your life.

My Good News Story

You have a faith story. You may never have reflected upon it to any great extent. You have an experience of life, which is different from that of any one else. Part of your story are moments of grace when you realised that God was with you. It may have evoked a generosity in you which led you into a deeper trust in him. You may be able to remember that precise time. Your enthusiasm may have waned somewhat, but yet it had a profound impact upon you.

As you reflect, you may possibly recall two ways in which you see the action of God in your life. Firstly, the time you knew that the Christian story was real and true for you and not simply for others. It became a moment of decision when you decided to give a greater place to God in your life. The guidelines given below are drawn up with that moment in mind. They will help you to clarify your story and recall the circumstances and the changes it led to for you.

Secondly, the many times when you knew that God was helping you through difficult situations. These guidelines can also help you to learn of God's guidance, wisdom and support for you that you have possibly known throughout your life. Looking again at these times will serve to deepen your faith and trust in God.

The great value of this exercise is that you will know that you have a story to relate, which no one else can contradict, simply because it is yours. Should you ever wish to tell your story it will leave a profound impact. It is really the story of God active, living and making a difference in your life. It needs to be told in a way that is sensitive to the situation of the hearer, in a language and a manner which is genuinely your own, without seeking to impress. It is best related in your own words and without religious jargon for the sake of making it seem impressive.

Decide now on a time and day when you will complete the exercise below and set out your own story. Write it as a continuation of your time of prayer on a day of your choosing.

There are three parts in putting together your story. Be specific and give real examples as you complete this exercise.

(a) Describing aspects of the way you lived and the way you saw things before the event.
- What was your life like before you came to know Christ in a more personal way?
- What were some of your attitudes? your values? your questions? your difficulties?
- What took up all your time? What did you give all your thinking time to?
- Where did you seek security and contentment?

(b) The actual change and what led to it.
- What led to your deepening trust in Christ? Why did you decide to take this step at that particular time?
- What were your reactions when faced with this decision?
- Describe the precise moment of change for you. When and in what circumstances did you come to a deeper trust in Christ?

(c) The way things are for you since that time.
There is often the temptation to over exaggerate and to see everything as wonderful. It is important to be aware of the real situation of your life with its continuing

questions and difficulties, while knowing the provi-
dence and action of God.
- What changes did you see in your life? in your actions? in your attitudes?
- When did you recognise that changes were taking place in your life?
- Who is Jesus Christ for you now and what is his influ-ence in your life?

We recommend that you write out the answers to the above. When completed it should take about three min-utes to read it. You now have a 'Good News Story' should you ever wish to stand up and tell it before a group or in an one-to-one conversation.

This exercise is purely for yourself so that you may be-come more sensitive to the action of God, who has been, and is always, at work in your life. It will be completely at your discretion if you ever wish to share it with another.

'From eternity God has thought of us and has loved us as unique individuals. He has called every one of us by name ... However, only in the unfolding of the history of our lives and its events is the eternal plan of God revealed to each of us ... a gradual process ... that happens day by day.'
(*Christifideles Laici* by Pope John Paul II)

Where do we go from here?

This course has always had a great impact upon those who have participated. From the six people cited at the beginning of this book, we have got a taste of its influence upon individuals. The course was first run in Ballinteer, Dublin, as a Lenten programme in 1990. It was then of seven weeks' duration. Its purpose was to inspire a more living faith. It included all the elements of the present course, prayer, reading of a scripture, song, a teaching and small group discussion. During the time together, a happy sense of community developed. Many spoke afterwards of the new beginning it was for them in their relationship with God and in becoming aware of what the church had to offer. Most of those participating had never attended any faith instruction since they left school and their only involvement was at the Sunday Mass, and for some not even that. A few were later to comment that fellow drinkers in the local pub would be very surprised when they learned of their attendance at a religious event.

The first course in Ballinteer proved to be a most happy and inspiring event. We were not prepared for what happened at the end. People wanted more. They liked what they had experienced. They wished to continue. Forty-six participated. Twenty-eight formed themselves into four small groups and arranged to meet in four available homes. During the course, we had learned of a parish cell system of evangelisation in St Boniface, Florida, and which had now arrived in Milan. A month after the four groups first met, four from Ballinteer travelled to Milan to see what was happening at first hand. We liked what we saw. We knew we had to adapt it to the Irish culture and mentality. We reported back to those meeting in the groups. They liked what they heard. Cell groups had been born in Ireland. During the following seven years they were joined by more than 250 fellow parishioners.

A Vision of Parish

A cell group is described in the Leader's Manual from St Boniface as 'an *oikos*-related, multiplying small group that seeks to evangelise, disciple, and shepherd through daily relationships'. It is the interaction of four to twelve people in a group setting, knowing that 'where two or three meet in my name, I shall be there with them' (Mt 18:20). It is a prayer experience. They encounter the Risen Lord among them and the principal question they bring before him and before one another is how can one's faith impact the relationships that are part of life.

Being *oikos*-related is central to the cell concept. *Oikos* is the Greek word for household or a house of people. It is often used in scripture to denote the extended family. It suggests those with whom we are in daily contact, those in the home, in the neighbourhood, in the places of work and leisure, in the school and in the shopping malls. This is our area of missionary activity. We don't need to go elsewhere to evangelise. Rather we evangelise as we go. Opportunities to share faith surround us each day. It may be as little as saying to someone in great difficulty that s/he will be remembered in our prayers, or helping a child to understand the religious programme. It may simply be to encourage another to pray about a particular situation. On occasion there will be more evangelistic moments when one shares one's personal faith story and may even lead another in prayer for a deeper awakening of God's love. Moments to encourage faith present themselves to everyone. The cell groups exists to help people to be alert to

such moments, to train people to be sensitive and respect-
ful in sharing with another, and to support them to have
the courage to speak when it is correct to do so.

To be Catholic is to have a concern that your faith be at
times seen and heard. This is not something that comes
easily and naturally. We have left it to others. We have understood missionary activity as what happens in third
world countries. It comes more easily to us to see faith as
private and not only as personal. In fact we share a suspi-
cion that to raise issues of faith is somewhat 'dangerous' as
it may lead to argument. Then we may not have answers
to the questions presented and will only show up our lack
of understanding. And so we need help. The cell group exists to help people towards sharing faith in a confident and
sensitive way within the network of their relationships.
The cell is about each individual availing of such help.
Hence there is practically no emphasis on membership but
rather on being fellow pilgrims, each seeking help and inspiration.

Cell groups present an exciting vision for a parish. It is
where everyone is an evangelist. Each person is seen as
having an important contribution to make. Each is called
to share in its mission. Each is called to a living faith. Faith
and mission are nurtured within small groups. A sense of
community develops as people meet together. They learn
of one another's strengths and weaknesses. When they are
strong they offer gratitude to God and support to others.
When weak, they seek prayer and assistance. They learn
the meaning of church as worship and as giving and receiving. For them the gospel 'works'. They see it in action.
They witness it in the way they relate together as well as in
their prayer. Yet this is only the beginning. They look outwards. Their meetings often conclude with the Our Father
as they hold hands and face outwards upon the world.
This is the world God loves. They are now being sent into
it to be his presence. They will seek to achieve this by their

love for, and acceptance of, everyone they meet. 'They will always have their answer ready for people who ask them the reason for the hope that they have' (1 Pet 3:15). They understand this as a way of loving, of pointing another to where s/he too can find true love and security. Sharing of faith is most credible where there is already a love relationship.

At their public worship, when they come together as a parish on Sunday, there will be great celebration. They have 'seen' the Lord in those in need and in all their relationships and the events of the week. This they want to celebrate. They will know that anything they achieve is God's work. There will be attentive listening to the Word of God and eager petitionary prayer. They know they need help and direction to continue to be pilgrim witnesses for the Lord. They know they need feeding at the table of the Lord.

I will let a few, who are involved in cell groups, offer an aspect of what this vision means for them:

One came to an appreciation of the work of priests:

'I always felt the priests were there and their function was to tell us what we were supposed to do and where we were going wrong and that they had all the answers. The cells have made me more aware of the tremendous work that so many priests are doing – definitely I would not have tuned into that.'

There is a void filled:

'As a married or single person in the church, there is no spiritual nourishment like retreats, unless you decide to do something yourself. There is a void in the nourishing of faith. I thank God that I attend a cell. Without it I know I would be going to Mass only for the kids' sake.'

The scriptures are opened:

'Most Catholics don't read the Bible because you

thought that was for the priest and he would tell you on Sunday morning. Hearing it from lay people and the understanding they have, gives you confidence that you could get understanding as well as they can. Otherwise I would never pick up a Bible. I now see it as God's love letter to me. I don't think Catholics in general pick up a Bible and read it. It was taboo, wasn't it?'

It has brought evangelisation into focus for another:

'The big change for me is the urgency to go out and tell others how I feel about God. In the beginning I was a bit impatient that they couldn't feel the same. We really need to get people connected to Jesus. People are crying out for it.'

Another has experienced the support of a community:

'My life has changed through the cells because I now have so many true friends. I had a bereavement on Christmas Eve and the support from the cells was unbelievable. After six months people still come and ask if things are OK. When you have something on your mind, you can go to people and you know that they will not turn you away. You know that you can speak to them in confidence and it will not be spread all over the parish. It has also opened up a whole new life for me.'

A new beginning in listening to others talking about Jesus in their lives:

'I just sat there but it was very peaceful. It was great to listen to others. There was something about all of us gathered together that was lovely. I hadn't a clue what I was letting myself in for. I went because I was invited. I knew nobody in the room except the girl who asked me to attend. When I saw the way the group reacted, I knew that there must be something good about it. I felt drawn back. There was some-thing there that was different, that nobody had offered me before. Nobody has ever shared their personal religion with me. The best you'd ever get of a personal sharing was over a pint in a pub when they were on the third or fourth pint. I found it comforting to hear how lay people live their lives and cope with problems, and how Jesus is in their lives and how this helps them through crises.'

Fr Joe Delaney, PP, Callan, Co Kilkenny has already introduced cell groups and plans to make their development the parish contribution to the millennium. He comments: 'It has given me the support of a group with whom I can share faith. For me it is family. The experience of seeing people discover Jesus in the gospel deepens my faith. Of all the projects I have heard for the renewal of the church, cell groups hold the best hope.'

Fruit of the cell experience in Ballinteer:
Once people began to pray, to think evangelisation, and to share together, many unforeseen spin-offs emerged. They included:
(a) The young adults formed teams. They sought to communicate their message through song, mime, dance, puppets, etc. They put together a programme and travelled, on invitation, to many places sharing their faith with others.
(b) People were trained to visit door to door on behalf of the parish. They offer a greeting from the parish and, where appropriate, a word of faith. They act as a reminder of the local parish community to all they visit.
(c) A children's church project was initiated through the efforts of young parents.
(d) A male choral group of thirty strong was formed and have performed a number of concerts.
(e) Leadership Training Courses are hosted to com-

municate skills and techniques for those wishing to set up faith-sharing groups. More than 200 people throughout Ireland have availed of these courses.
(f) People take responsibility for their own faith development, and many avail of theology diplomas and degrees, as well as personal enrichment and scripture courses.

These are but a flavour of what has emerged in the parish of Ballinteer, once people had availed of an 'internship', of a few years of learning within the cell community. The distinctive quality is that people take a responsibility for these activities, in collaboration with the parish teams of the local parishes, without adding greatly to the workload of clergy. Any parish which takes on small faith groups as part of a parish plan can expect to witness their own distinctive outreaches and activities emerge.

Remember, you are always welcome to contact the author or the Ballinteer Cell Community for further information or advice.